SO-AFT-826

Jazz, Rags & Blues

9 original pieces for the late intermediate pianist

MARTHA MIER

Jazz is an important and distinctive American contribution to 20th-century music. *Jazz, Rags and Blues*, Book 4, contains nine original solos that reflect the various styles of the jazz idiom. From the slow blues swing style of "Last Chance Blues" to the bright and happy jazz sound of "Mr. Trumpet Man," students will love the challenge of playing in the jazz style.

Jazz is fun to play! Students will be inspired and motivated by the syncopated rhythms and the colorful, rich harmonies of jazz—a style which has captured the imagination of performer and listener alike!

Alfred

for Kaitlyn Alexandra

Katy's Dance

Martha Mier

STEAMBOAT RAG

Martha Mier

Moderately, with a steady beat (play ♪ evenly)

Last Chance Blues

Martha Mier

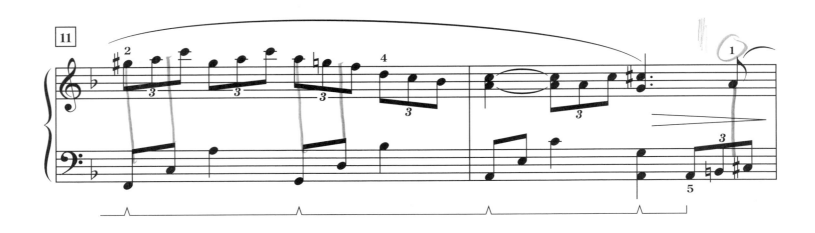

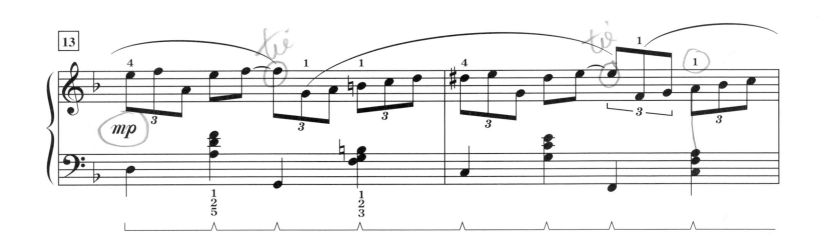

Mr. Trumpet Man

Martha Mier

for Laurie Readout

Grandview Boulevard Strut

Martha Mier

Tuxedo Jazz

Martha Mier

Jauntily ♫ = ♪♪ (♩ = 120)

GOOD TIME RAG

Martha Mier

Lively, with a steady beat (play ♪♪ evenly)

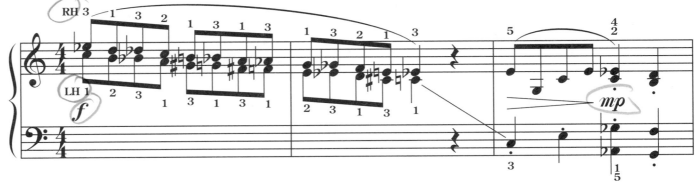

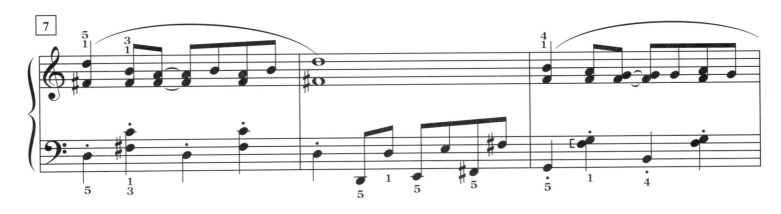

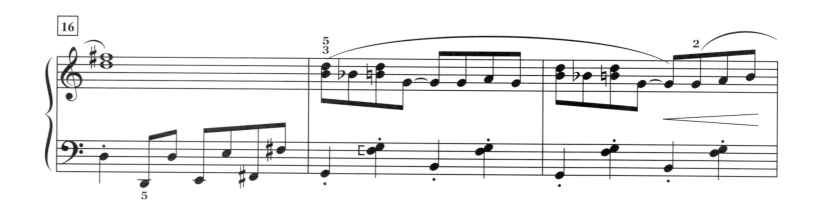

Jackson Street Blues

Martha Mier

Easy relaxed tempo ♪♪ = ♪³♪ (♩ = 76)

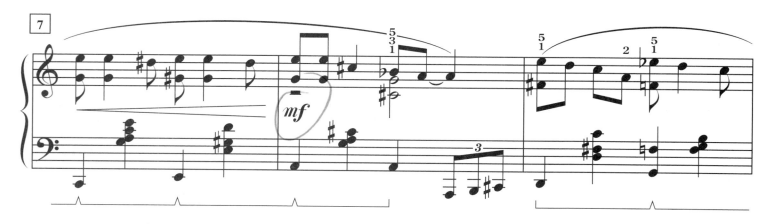

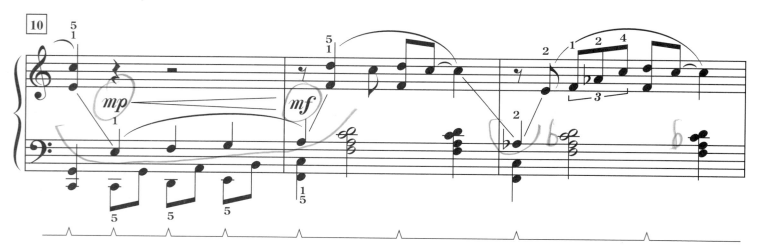

for Ken and Lourdes

Birmingham Blues

Martha Mier